The Boy Born With A Pinhole Heart

poems by

Keith Mark Gaboury

Finishing Line Press
Georgetown, Kentucky

The Boy Born With
A Pinhole Heart

Copyright © 2022 by Keith Mark Gaboury
ISBN 978-1-64662-991-6 First Edition
All rights reserved under International and Pan-American Copyright Conventions. No part of this book may be reproduced in any manner whatsoever without written permission from the publisher, except in the case of brief quotations embodied in critical articles and reviews.

ACKNOWLEDGMENTS

Grateful acknowledgements are made to the following journals in which these poems originally appeared or are forthcoming:

Little Stone Journal: "Dementia Descends"
Manzano Mountain Review: "I Awoke"
Rumble Fish Quarterly: "The Man I Am Not" (Retitle)

Publisher: Leah Huete de Maines
Editor: Christen Kincaid
Cover Art: Keith Mark Gaboury; Family Photograph; 1930s; Brest, France
Author Photo: Jacob Gaboury
Cover Design: Elizabeth Maines McCleavy

Order online: www.finishinglinepress.com
also available on amazon.com

Author inquiries and mail orders:
Finishing Line Press
PO Box 1626
Georgetown, Kentucky 40324
USA

Table of Contents

Home 1

The Boy Born With a Pinhole Heart 2

He Returned 3

Cribbage 4

Dementia Descends 5

Neighborhood Knock 6

My Grandfather's Eulogy 7

The Man I Am Not 8

The Boy Who Sang With His Brother 10

The Boy Who Shielded Against Sunburns 11

Witness 12

I Awoke 13

My Father Told Her 14

We Live In This Universe 15

mother and son 17

I Breathe With My Grandparent's Ghosts 18

I Am A Face of Echoes 19

Family Time 21

A Boy No More 22

My Heart Is Now a Firm Hand 23

Breaking Anew 24

Dedicated To

Charles Francis Bryson (1918 – 2006)
Kevin P. Bryson (1955 – 2018)
Mary Beth Bryson (1955 – Living)
Bryse Gaboury (1980 – Living)
David Richard Gaboury (1953 – Living)
Dennis Gaboury (1951 – Living)
Jacob Richard Gaboury (1982 – Living)
Mary Elizabeth Gaboury (1954 – Living)
Annette E. Kerjean (1901 – 1985)
Madeleine Isabelle Rogers (1922 – 2008)
William Francis Rogers (1891 – 1972)
Dannette Velez (1971 – 2007)

Home

Sticking out my tongue for the prick of an October snow

Sitting by Danette's bedside as the disease tangles deeper into the soil of her body

Air vaulting out of my lungs from my brother's suckerpunch

Flipping over my pineapple cake into an upside down completion

Whispers weaving at Grace Methodist about how many weeks Danette has left

Soccer cleats clicking on our hardwood floor

Humidity fogging my glasses into blindness

Reading in adulthood Danette's online journal: tumors grew from her unborn egg

The Boy Born with a Pinhole Heart

Remember: he came out gasping
with a pinhole heart
dripping into the expanse
of his neonate body.

Heart cells
reborn every solar cycle
since he breathed in an incubator
and we paced in hallway pain

over days that leaked into darkness
marked first by an absent moon
to a waxing gibbous climb.

Under an expanding glow,
the defection closed
like a sealed pipe
redeemed within a home
he's since claimed as his own.

The front door of his eyes
swung open
where we waited
by white gleaming chairs
under fluorescent glare.

He Returned

War still stabbed his muscles
into an open bleed

as he vaulted to a father of five
to children who only felt his horror
from the slap of his tongue

giving life to the memory
over boots stomping on blood
soaked into Belgian soil

sixty years before a plaque
went up in his honor
yet the metal reads Charles K.
when his birth certificate
reads Charles F.

who as a grandfather
sits in his leather chair's grip.

Cribbage

At my kitchen table in Boston,
the rush of shuffling
a 52-card deck sends me back

to my grandparent's home
where I sat with Grandpa Charles
at his maroon-stained table.

When I leaned over his cribbage board,
we found ritual
with a deck of cards

by dealing, cutting, scarifying
to peg up and down his board.
Before we ever shuffled at his table,

he knew the battle of losing
his brother to whiskey: slumped in a chair
like a comrade back at the Battle of the Bulge

slumped in mud as bullets found skin.
Away from blood, Charles flipped over
a Jack from the deck
onto his stained victory table.

Dementia Descends

An owl family descends upon
my grandfather's synaptic membrane

as he plants a period at his oak desk
on the first stanza of a villanelle
to a wife he only speaks to in the past tense.

Within neurons sparking consciousness,
the mama builds a nest

by raiding their first year of marriage
carved into the tree of his temporal lobe.

His skin and his shadow's skin
merge into one: he has no
history of anniversaries or births

to spring his words alive.
They stand hollow on the page

through a mind-sight link
consumed with owl infestation.

Every night, the papa hunts fresh prey
to bring back to the ravenous
in a cemetery of memory.

Neighborhood Knock

In the season that spiraled
to my grandfather's death,
his neighbor Nancy knocked on his door
every Sunday to play cribbage.

He couldn't remember the tomato soup
he slurped the same day—a winter sun
shining onto his red sustenance—
when dementia slaughtered
as a soldier, hacking neurons
before it sliced away pounds of muscle

yet he still knew how to gather his royal cards
for a Jack-Queen-King run
through the flesh of his WWII mind.

After each game, his wife
bathed his skeleton frame
in the sixtieth year of their marriage.
The winter before, he stood over her bed
and screamed into her sleeping face.

On one Sunday, Nancy smiled
with a January sun descending
on a gaunt man
ready to reveal his final four-card hand.

My Grandfather's Eulogy

After I wrote it
in Aunt Nancy's guest bedroom,
I went outside to breathe
under a basket of rain
on her warped back porch
as those words echoed
in the wet forest between my ears.

A sunrise later in St. Mark's Church,
it jutted beyond
the fallen eucalyptus of my tongue.
Uncle Kevin wrapped me
in a welder's squeeze-me-alive hug
when I returned to my family
smiling in a pew.

The Man I Am Not

After the life of Kevin Bryson (1955 - 2018)

By a tall fire I want to hug,
I know Cesium-137
traveled from Atomic Age detonation
into the water cycle.

Since marking residence
in my blood flow,
Cesium-137 says
snatch a family
to live as grass blades
mowed on a duplicated lawn.

By a shrinking fire I want to hug,
shadows tongue my face
like a bulldog
when the man I am not
swivels home into dinner arms.

No one waits for me
through a red-thick door
while Cesium-137
bombards on
I must slap on some flesh
to cutout wife and kids.
Cutout is never enough.

By a low fire I want to hug,
Cesium-137 only sees deficiency;
it does not know *my* history.
Look up! The Capricornus Constellation

stared down one light-year ago
upon my sister Elizabeth at 17
swerving to miss a neighborhood dog.
When she rammed into a street pole,
I capitulated headfirst through the windshield
onto Massachusetts gravel

as Elizabeth's bodiless screams
ballooned into our family calamity.
Where is my sister? Where is my sister?
still echoing.

With my once mighty fire
at a low ember, I trace my forehead scar.
Yes, Cesium-137 scratches within.
Can I bludgeon that radioactive haunt?
Give me a lifetime
and I'll give witness.

The Boy Who Sang With His Brother

After "We Real Cool" by Gwendolyn Brooks

Under a highway overpass, we
ran past an unhoused man who really
needed love but we needed to cool
off in Boston darkness so we

spat in each others' faces and left
our gum wrappers behind like school-
age children abandoned. On cracked concrete, we
gathered in the warmth of our shadows lurking
against returning to mother's whiskey breath, a late-

night split to Forest Hills called us where we
halted at the gate, struck
our feet over metal. Straight
to Grandpa Charles' grave, we
felt the etching on his stone, sang
his wedding song through the sinful

lyrics he smiled upon. Yes, we
flew high to swallow the city into our thin
souls: a mountain of moons and gin
awaited us, a friend we

say now. There in the bedroom we shared, a jazz
record played in the month our mother June
slunk back to Confession for sins we
didn't understand. She only died
last week. This story is still so freshly sown.

The Boy Who Shielded Against Sunburns

I taught my palest son
the reality of sunrays
slobbering his white

petal skin into a red pain
by the glee
of our neighborhood pool.

Under this punishment,
I slapped on that mass-
produced magic.
Rub it in all the way
so the white doesn't show
I commanded

before he tucked himself
into a cannon ball
and exploded into welcoming water.

If he felt dangerous, he'd open
his eyes to the pencil legs of kids
swinging through chlorine sting.

We arrived home with a towel
wrapped around his waist,
water soaking the doorstep,
and his body still white as a lily
in an island of flowers.

Witness

He held witness
to my afternoon hands
hanging my bra on the clothesline
as if placing a fallen nest
back on its native limb
against wind shaking one blue egg
like the egg his limbs sprang from
after a red robin chirped
outside my bedroom window
when I saw that stick go blue

I Awoke

to my father cursing
back when a Saturday
stretched out like film strip.

Adulthood stood oblong in shadow
as his *Fuck You* flung
disjointed into my bedroom's
soft skin. I peeked out my door

where he bent under
our kitchen sink, his hands
clawing at busted pipes.

With his toolbox open
like an unhinged jaw,
he reached for his screwdriver
but grabbed his hammer's force.

I walked over to hand him
his screwdriver and a smile
just to keep him moving
as a man should.

My Father Told Her

a gut punch of words
at our front door
while I watched Coyote chase Road Runner
with a steel knife and fork
on my Looney Tunes screen.

My mother's purse
thumped onto hardwood.
I sat before the animation of adolescence
where Coyote's parachute failed,
he swallowed Acme Aspirin
and fell onto arid ground.

My father's gut punch
didn't project within a TV frame
we could turn off
in our pillbox home
I only know from memory sketches.
Just as Coyote's fork vaulted up
to stab Road Runner meat,
my father called me over.

We leaned into a tight coil.
When I heard him declare
I lost my job, a ravenous animal
bursted upon us, yellow eyes
glaring at a fresh family kill.

We Live In This Universe

Over exposed lobster,
I sat with my father
in open Boston air

when he gathered the language—
in 1960 Attleboro, Massachusetts
his uncle Mark got *molested*

while Mark and my father
scored God points
as altar boys at Saint Mary's School.

Father James Porter glossed over
my father's five-year-old frame

and pinned a twelve-year-old Mark
among the thirty children

who all clamored
like lobsters boiled alive, unheard
behind a Catholic door.

In The Many Worlds Theory,
is there a multiverse
Porter pounced on my father's

boyhood, his body buckling
before he heaved
the weight of young marriage.

If I step through a wormhole
into this shivering reality,

would I still dine over cracked lobster
with his retired self

or stop Porter
from loosening his belt
within Saint Mary's walls?

We live in this universe:
Porter died of prostate cancer,

my parents celebrate
their anniversary every June,

and Mark walks past Saint Mary
of the Immaculate to work.

Last year, his name got printed
in <u>The Globe</u>. Everyone knows

but they only hand him
their smiles.

mother and son

i'm a basketcase
just so you know

i know

you don't want me
at the restaurant
moping around

could you call
your therapist tomorrow

i don't have time for that

what do you mean
of course you do

we have a trip planned

that's one thing
you can do this

i'm going back to bed

will you call her tomorrow

tomorrow is the first anniversary
of kevin's death

and your brother would want you to call

ok

I Breathe With My Grandparent's Ghosts

In the marrow of their bedroom,
I find them alive

where Madeleine's perfume
waves hello. I am a visitor
to the residency of her pillbox hat

atop the red oak dresser
she loved as if her blood
stained the wood.

I turn towards the Bronze Star
Charles earned in Belgium
hanging in a black frame.

After he read *Night*,
he stepped into his garden
with tears etched on his cheeks

like the tattoos
branded onto Final Solution skin.

In their kitchen, I see Madeleine
cooking her 1995 Easter ham
in her wedgewood oven.

At their front door, I'm shaking
Charles' hand
while dementia genocides his mind

a new century after Auschwitz,
January 1945. That same month,
he earned his Bronze Star

I now clutch
under a Massachusetts lamplight.

I Am a Face of Echoes

My grandmother's smile
undying
atop her autumn leaf dresser.

I'm watching myself
step inside this 1932 photograph
to be alongside
her teenage self on a family vacation.

I only knew her
as a grandmother who lived
with Charles on Fairway Drive.

beside Mount Hope Cemetery
where her bones scream white
in a language I listen to
when I visit the grass
growing over her body.

Last winter, I pressed
my palm on her tombstone.
In my pocket, I felt the photograph

of her in 1932 Brest, France
toasting with a wine glass
alongside relatives I only know by name.

I've now snatched a glass
to talk and laugh
with Madeleine Bryson

before she married Charles
or swallowed 1960s whiskey
or latched sight
upon her first grandchild.

Before all that, what words
will she offer
to my face of echoes:
a Bryson blend
on the soil of our heritage.

Family Time

Three coffees and one lunar rise
since I cried, stripped back
into a dry husk.

My mother's words
echo into a chant: she demanded a new brain,
not the depressed one given at birth.

In her birthright, she screamed
from her hospice lock
until our family gathered
into a hive of funeral handshakes.

Under a lamp's shine,
I stare at a 1957 snapshot
that distills my mother as a little girl
with her grandmother Annette
both hugging Breton dolls.

French hands popped in fake sockets,
stitched white rose dresses
with a cap secured by a strap.

These porcelain faces crossed waves
to reach backyard sunlight
captured in black and white time.

I can't sit too long in memory.
I put on my star-watching socks
in search of moonlight
that will wrap me into a hug.

A Boy No More

I stream past the library
where I once screamed in the quiet

after my Pop Rocks dropped,
sending out a shock wave

I couldn't lasso back. As my mother
shoveled at me a December stare,

I scampered outside with fifteen cents
jangling in my jeans pocket

yet I only needed ten
for another sugar bomb

under a mean sun
dumping radiation like candy.

The same Boston sun
smacks down a July wallop.

Sweating in a web-thin layer of cotton,
I turn away from that library facade

to dance my talking tongue
before a bartender friend

who pours kissing shots of Jameson
that stings my throat like a garden spider.

My garden is on a barstool
with my tab growing like a hungry vine.

My Heart Is Now a Firm Hand

I trip off a 38 bus.
Whiskey leaps in my blood.
A rabbit in a lettuce patch.
I'll never see that. I only see
green in Safeway.
I cut to the alcohol aisle
on a Wednesday night.

Handle swings on Taylor Street
through the Tenderloin. Back as a boy
my mother once said
your heart is like tender meat.
My heart is now a firm hand
welcoming a 86-proof friend.

Breaking Anew

Dawn peels back night's skin
to reveal the organs of a new day.

I step into a salt welcome
where the Pacific Ocean
froths at my feet.

With my mother's
body still fresh in the ground,

I sought whiskey's warmth
under the rise and collapse
of a lunar cycle.

When the moon abandoned the sky,
a black expanse showed no solace

to bloodshot eyes
seeing my future

in my mother's martini body
degenerating into a cold bed.

At midnight, I screamed at a family
of naked stars
shining onto waves breaking anew.

After he grew up in the Bay Area, Castle Rock, Colorado, and Olathe, Kansas, **Keith Mark Gaboury** earned a B.A. in English: Concentration in Creative Writing from Baker University, a M.A. in English from San Francisco State University, and a M.F.A. in Creative Writing from Emerson College. His poetry has appeared in such literary publications as *Poetry Quarterly*, *New Millennium Writings*, and *Map Literary*. Duck Lake Books published his chapbook *Hello Universe Lovers* (2020) and The Pedestrian Press published *Oakland, I'm Not Dead* (2020). While he writes in free verse, form, and prose poetry, his poetry ranges from the surreal, historical, and present-day urban reality. Keith is a Pushcart-nominated poet, preschool teacher, and runner in Oakland, California. Learn more at *www.keithmgaboury.com*.

www.ingramcontent.com/pod-product-compliance
Lightning Source LLC
LaVergne TN
LVHW041520070426
835507LV00012B/1706